TANKERS ON BRITISH ROADS

CARL JOHNSON

AMBERLEY

First published 2022

Amberley Publishing
The Hill, Stroud
Gloucestershire, GL5 4EP

www.amberley-books.com

Copyright © Carl Johnson, 2022

The right of Carl Johnson to be identified as
the Author of this work has been asserted in
accordance with the Copyrights, Designs and
Patents Act 1988.

ISBN 978 1 3981 0078 7 (print)
ISBN 978 1 3981 0079 4 (ebook)

British Library Cataloguing in Publication Data.
A catalogue record for this book is available from
the British Library.

Origination by Amberley Publishing.
Printed in the UK.

Acknowledgements

A lorry fan for most of my life, I could not have managed to capture some of the vehicles included here without the help of friends and fellow members of a number of clubs that I have been involved with.

These people have added information, guided me to locations and even accompanied me on photo expeditions including trips abroad and to many shows and operators' yards, etc.

Thanks then to the following: George Barker, Ian Moxon, Malcolm Mortimer, Neil Matlock, Raymond Jenkins, the late Steve Wimbush, Michael Marshall, John Andrew, the late Gary Russell, Nigel Scaife, my old boss Arthur Shirley, Barry Randall, John Heath, Mike Waudby, Nigel Bunt, Peter Davies, Peter Seaword, Richard Stanier, John Salisbury and to all the operators, owner drivers and companies that have afforded me time and allowed me to take the photographs.

To any I have missed I apologise. On my travels I have come across many individuals that may have made contributions, be it in depth or just added snippets of information. I am forever in their debt.

Introduction

Road tankers come in many forms. The carriage of certain goods and products very often dictates the type, shape and overall appearance.

Industry has adapted to many innovations over the years and we have powder tanks, tanks for liquids and even specialised tanks for the carriage of a plethora of goods from live eels to animal feed, cement, plastic pellets, chemicals, etc.

All of the photographs depicted in this book have been taken with the author's own camera over a number of years. It is hoped that the reader enjoys browsing through them as much as the author did taking them, thus capturing on film and recording an important part of our transport history.

Tankers on British Roads

Tanks for everything; no pun intended but a statement of fact, as today so many commodities, raw and finished materials, are carried in bulk tankers.

Over the years technology has advanced in many areas including the transporting of goods in bulk, from milk to fuel in liquid form and to dry powders and pellets with air blown discharge systems.

Specialised tankers have also been developed for the carriage of live fish and eels.

Transporting in tankers can be traced back to the horse and cart days, with sanitation and water being an early priority.

As motor transport evolved and the demand for fuel and oil increased, the use of the ubiquitous 2-gallon can was very much in vogue. Alas the sheer manpower involved for this antiquated method soon saw the road tanker coming on stream.

Bulk fuel tanks at filling stations were a major step forward, and road tanks were soon to be seen conveying the products of heavy oil (diesel), motor spirit (petrol), paraffin, tractor vaporising oil (TVO) and lubricating oils.

Refineries were strategically placed around the shores of Great Britain. These were to convert the crude oil into the various products to service the network of outlets, which included many industries, and a growing network of retail filling stations.

Another vital labour-intensive commodity was the transporting of milk. The handling of churns between farms and dairies with the resultant cleansing and sterilising was very time consuming.

However, the use of churns lived on for many years, and the railways were one of the first to recognise the potential in moving milk in bulk, with railheads and sidings being located at many dairies.

The milk would be transported to major cities and bottled locally for the then popular service of doorstep deliveries to most households.

How times change as even the sight of a 'traditional' milkman is indeed rare today.

The labour needed at docks and warehouses for other products like flour in bags, tallow and oils in drums, etc, was another area that had to be improved by the reduction of manpower and providing a better infrastructure by installing holding tanks, silos and offloading facilities.

Tallow is used in products including soap and cosmetics, as well as candles. Nowadays this is carried in bulk in insulated tankers, as are other 'heavy' oils and fats that need to be kept fluid.

When these products have been discharged by pressure pump the tankers are purged with steam to clean them out. Any residue left can soon set, which makes it harder to remove.

Some readers may see the letters SCOPA on the rear of a number of tankers followed by numbers. This is to show that the tanker is dedicated to the carriage of food products. SCOPA stands for the Seed Crushers and Oil Processors Association and the numbers will be the operators registration number.

The SCOPA-registered users agree to maintain high standards of maintenance and cleanliness, even down to the traceability of flexible hoses.

Another sign often seen on tankers (and sometimes other vehicles) are the 'Hazchem' signs. This is really an 'action' code for personnel like the emergency services to provide information on what load is carried, and an emergency telephone number is provided so the relevant procedures are used in the event of a mishap or spillage with help and advice from the product manufacturers.

Other liquids carried in bulk are that vital commodity H2O, or water to the man in the street, add malt and hops to that and we have beer, another product transported by tankers. Some pubs having bulk holding tanks, having said that the good old barrel still reigns supreme.

Powders like flour and cement are also discharged by compressing the tanker and as these are very fine products they actually flow almost like water. The majority of powders are usually aided for discharge by tipping up the tank body.

The use of plastics in the modern age means the demand for plastic pellets has increased and these are again discharged at customers premises by compressed air, which are used in the manufacture of a great number of products from bottles to car components.

The majority of these photographs were taken in what I consider to be the twilight years of the British transport industry before we saw the disappearance of the UK lorry manufacturers.

An avid fan of the British lorry, it may come as no surprise that few foreign vehicles are included in this book. We all have our favourites but mine was ERF from the neighbouring county of Cheshire and therefore these have more than their fair share of exposure.

Back in those days there was often surprises turning up, from old vehicles still capable of a good hard day's graft to the operator rebuilds and conversions that nowadays, due to strict regulations, seem to have died a death.

The information in the captions is as far as possible accurate. Hopefully it is not too technical but gives a general overview. If any mistakes have crept in they are entirely of my own making and I take full responsibility for this.

A picture paints a thousand words so goes the saying, so have a browse and enjoy.

Back in June 1992 a visit to Turners (Soham) Ltd was undertook, and this smart-looking ERF E10 with Cummins 290 engine is seen in the yard at Fordham, Ely. It is coupled to a British Sugar-liveried tri-axle tank trailer. The discharge equipment can be seen mounted at the front of the tank.

Another ERF E10 articulated sugar tanker of Turners. This time the unit is in the British Sugar livery as well. With the well-known brand name of 'Silver Spoon', the company is a major supplier both in the retail and wholesale markets. Turners went onto grow into a major operator, having made several acquisitions over the years.

Seen in 1989 at the yard of Nelstrop's Flour at Albion Mills, Lancashire Hill, Stockport, this Foden Fleetmaster with the Mk1 S10 cab has a Cummins engine fitted and has had the addition of a tag axle on the unit.

Less than twelve months later the outfit had been resprayed into Nelstrop's white livery. Seen on 5 August 1990, the vehicle was still giving good service even at nine years old and was used to distribute flour throughout the UK.

On the same visit in 1990 it was nice to see this 1973 registered AEC Mammoth Major, also still in daily use. The Sankey Ergomatic cab still seemed to be in good order and luckily this lorry did make it into the realms of preservation.

Even better for an avid ERF fan was to see 'The Silkworm', a 1967 ERF 68GX. Chassis number 14909 was new to King Bros (Carriers), who later went into the Allied Mills empire. The vehicle also went into preservation, with the tank interior actually being fitted out as living quarters!

Keen-eyed enthusiasts will spot that this T45 cabbed unit is badged as a Scammell Roadtrain, which is of course correct. However, as part of the Leyland Motors Group the Leyland name is far more prominent. Again, it is seen in Nelstrop's yard in 1990.

This ERF E10 artic was spotted on Cartmill Services near Yeovil in Somerset when on a southern 'safari'. The company had a variety of tankers and this particular one was for the carriage of liquid fertiliser. Lurking behind was another similar vehicle, both resting while the drivers took their mandatory break.

Ace Tip also had a depot in Wareham, Dorset, where we came upon this ERF C Series artic slurry tanker. The strange looking building behind is almost out of a science fiction film. As this is a local registered vehicle, it might be safe to assume it was supplied by Frank Tucker of Exeter.

Although a lot of photographs in this book are from earlier decades, we have here a later shot from 2007. A rather nice-looking MAN TGA artic powder tanker of Street's from Cranage. It had just loaded at Bathgate Silica Sand in Arclid, Sandbach, and grossed at 44 tons.

On the same day, and brand new at Arclid Transport, this Volvo FM480 is seen here coupled to a hired tank trailer from WG Tanker Hire (Waterhouses Garage). More on Waterhouses Garage later on.

A company that unfortunately no longer exists is Barlow & Hodgkinson Ltd, from the small hamlet of Biggin by Hartington near Buxton. Not a very large fleet they were engaged on limestone traffics from nearby quarries. This Foden Haulmaster S10 Mk1 is a typical workhorse.

Another of Barlow & Hodgkinson's seen enjoying a weekend rest in the yard, another Foden but this time an articulated tipping powder tanker. It is a model S106T with a double drive rear bogie and twin wheels, some of these had super single tyres fitted.

A fine E10 ERF articulated tanker for the carriage of bulk powders as proclaimed quite boldly on the front of this A. M. Bell's vehicle. It was seen in their yard way back in 1991 having just returned after a week's work.

'Salty' and his trusty steed, a DAF CF85-430, seen parked ready to exit the Cemex Quarry in Doveholes in April 2005. A. M. Bell no longer run any vehicles but retain a DAF parts dealership. The onsite testing station for HGVs and PSVs is still operational.

Bituminous Road Facilities Ltd (BRF) had a number of vehicles in the yard at Henstridge, Somerset, that were out of use and looking well past their sell by date when visited in 1993. This unidentified AEC Mammoth Major tar emulsion tanker was such an example.

Seddon Atkinson 401 eight-wheel emulsion tanker/sprayer, also at BRF, was another that had probably come to the end of the road. These tar tankers were insulated to keep the tar fluid, enabling them to spray the road before stone chippings were added.

Dating from 1972, this Foden S39 eight-wheel tanker had also been used as a sprayer. However, we thought that as the pump and pipework had been altered it may have been used as a buffer storage facility (you can see the extension and connection just to the side). Unfortunately, there was no one around to ask for any information, so its pure conjecture!

You may ask what on earth is Boral Pozzolan? Well, it is actually a by-product from power stations, namely fly-ash. It is added to concrete to increase flow and strength. This DAF 2500 eight-wheeler powder tanker was seen parked one weekend in Leek, Staffordshire, and was operated by Mitchell Cotts.

Another Mitchell Cotts vehicle, this Leyland DAF 95 artic powder tanker was captured on film at a Mitchell Cotts depot on the Penkridge Industrial Estate. The company was bought out by Transfleet in July 1988.

Fleet number 83803 on the hymn sheet at Calor, Kings Lynn. This ERF E10 tractor unit with a rest cab is coupled to a tri-axle tank trailer. The photograph was taken on 27 June 1992 after being allowed access by the then manager of the depot – quite a privilege!

At the other end of the scale and still in Kings Lynn depot we see another ERF, this time a four-wheel rigid E6 with a day cab. Fleet number 21190 would have been used to service domestic and small commercial outlets with Liquid Petroleum Gas (LPG).

Something of a 'scoop' was to gain access to the Longbridge Hayes (Stoke) depot of Carless Refining and Marketing. This Foden 4300, fleet number 203, was one of several seen on the day but a 'working' shot always wins the day.

This ERF B Series coupled to an ex-Wincanton tar emulsion tanker was the yard shunter in the Carless depot. The original Carless, Capel & Leonard company were responsible for 'inventing' the word petrol.

Originally this Foden Haulmaster was with ECC Quarries and had an S10 Mk1 cab. It was sold to Glutton Bridge Garage, who traded as Buxton Aggregates and stationed the lorries at Harpur Hill. During this time, it was fitted with an S10 Mk2 cab as seen here in the yard in 1995.

ERF C31 eight-wheel tar tanker of Colas seen in the yard at Exeter way back in 1991. Colas is an international company with approximately twenty UK locations and are a major player in road resurfacing and airfield applications.

The AEC Marshal lorries were much favoured by Colas at one time. This was due to them being able to maintain a low speed with decent engine revolutions, ideal for the job in hand of spraying hot tar emulsion. This resulted in long service, and this one, still in use in 1991, was already sixteen years old.

Still with Colas in Exeter, we see here another C Series ERF, this time a C40 articulated insulated tar tanker. It was used to transfer hot tar emulsion from the depot to major jobs where the emulsion would be transferred to the sprayer vehicles prior to laying down road chippings.

Seen just over the border in Dorset, on the Weymouth bypass, was an Exeter-based Foden Haulmaster S10 Mk1 six-wheel tar sprayer. Originally registered in Hull, the lorry was alongside a later Foden 4250 patiently waiting for the next job.

Still with Colas but moving over to Hampshire, we see here in the Andover depot a Hants-registered ERF A Series 4x2 unit coupled to the ubiquitous tar tank trailer. Again, longevity was the order of the day as this lorry was just short of its twentieth birthday.

Foden S106T 6x4 tractor unit coupled to a powder tanker for the carriage of calcium carbonate (limestone). The product is very versatile and can be found as a food additive as well as in use as agricultural lime. The vehicle, owned by Croxton & Garry from Matlock, was caught taking a rest at the Ferrybridge Service area just off the M62 and A1.

At the Starbeck depot (Harrogate) of Dairy Products we see here a Leyland (T45 cab) drawbar milk tanker. Badged as a Constructor 24-21, it may have been a conversion or a recab as normally Constructors were multi-axle six- or eight-wheel rigid vehicles.

DAF 2300 6-wheel milk tanker also seen in the Starbeck depot. The company was formerly known as Dairy Crest and prior to that the Milk Marketing Board. Several outfits here were kitted out for drawbar operation.

Still on the theme of milk, we have a fine-looking AEC Mammoth Major of J & E Dickinson (Longley Farm) of Holmfirth, Yorkshire. Another good example of longevity as the vehicle was almost nineteen years old when seen in 1991. Fortunately, this lorry is now in preservation.

A little younger than its AEC stablemate at Dickinson's, this Leyland Octopus eight-wheel milk tanker was used every day on bulk farm collections. Both lorries have door stickers that promote 'Real Dairy Cream', which is processed on site.

Bearing chassis number 48899 is one of a number of ERF lorries that were operated on the J & E Dickinson fleet. At this time the majority of the fleet were from this still (at the time) independent manufacturer. This one is a C Series with a day cab fitted and coupled to a tandem axle tank trailer.

One of the youngsters on the Dickinson's fleet was this two-year-old ERF E10 (rest cab) on chassis number 61690. This fine articulated outfit differs slightly from the previous photo as it is coupled to a tri-axle trailer riding on super single wheels and tyres.

An essential piece of equipment at a local boat hire company was this Ford/Iveco Cargo gully emptier. It was used not only on the hire fleet but also as a service to passing canal users to pump out the on-board waste tanks. Affectionately named 'Lavender Ginger', it was based in Stone, Staffordshire.

A number of fuel companies used contract hire vehicles for the distribution of their products. This ERF E10 (rest cab), fleet number 6048, was owned by United Transport, seen on the Sandbach M6 service area taking a break between deliveries on behalf of Esso.

In true fleet colours we have here fleet number 2678 of United Transport. Keen-eyed readers may spot the reference to part of the B.E.T. Group. British Electric Traction had a 20 per cent interest in United. The ERF E10 sleeper cab unit is coupled to tank number 5877 in the livery of Cargill, a major customer.

In full livery to Cargill with just the headboard reference to United Transport is another ERF E10 artic tanker. This was captured on Markham Moor Services just off the A1 near to Retford, Notts.

Full Cargill livery again but sporting fleet number 2201 is this sleeper cabbed DAF 2500 eight-wheel tanker of United Transport, also taking a break at Markham Moor. Cargill are a major supplier to the food and agriculture industries.

Back to milk and we see parked at home in the yard at Dunton Wharf, Curdworth, a Scania 93H (day cab) six-wheel two-compartment tanker of W. Freeman & Sons Ltd. The vehicle was on contract to Central Midlands Dairies, which is a co-operative of milk producers.

Brand new and fresh out of the box, this ERF ES6 180 (Steyr cab) single compartment tanker awaits its first turn of duty for Freeman's. Although registered, it had not been taxed to go on the road. It even still has the plastic protective covering on the tank's front and rear panels.

Originally a tractor unit on for H & R Johnson (Richards Tiles), this Leyland Buffalo was converted and driven by the author on the carriage of water ground bone in slop form for the production of bone china. It was owned by Stuart, Roy & Co. Ltd of Cheadle, Staffordshire. The firm had recently been acquired by a company from Cornwall, hence the GR logo.

Later on, an ex-Weavers of Endon Leyland Freighter (T45) milk tanker was acquired by the parent company of Stuart Roy. By now the company had been renamed Goonvean Ceramic Materials Ltd, Goonvean being a reference to the Cornish China Clay base in St Austell.

Ex-Hinckley's Silica Sand (Tilcon), this Foden Haulmaster S10 Mk1 found its way into Derbyshire with second owner Hazlecroft Garage Ltd of Buxton, Derbyshire. Hazlecroft named their vehicles (at the time) and *Derbyshire Chieftain* was kindly pulled out of the line of vehicles for a photograph one Saturday afternoon.

Derbyshire Grenadier was another Hazlecroft three-compartment powder tanker on contract to Buxton Lime Products (B.L.I.) for cement transport. The ERF E10 rest cab eight-wheeler was seen just having discharged it's load one Saturday morning in Swadlincote, Derbyshire.

The motto of Heygates Flour is 'Quality Tells' and yes, it does, when you see such a smartly turned-out outfit such as this ERF E10 rest cab artic. Fleet number 223 was photographed in the yard at Downham Market, a town on the edge of the fens in Norfolk.

Being both an ERF and drawbar fan, outfits like this are bound to face the author's camera. From Trafford Park, Manchester, Houghton Vaughan Plc are involved in the production of chemicals. This stunning combination was seen on the northbound service area of Keele services on the M6 motorway.

M6 services again, but this time Sandbach. A Reliance E12 ERF unit fleet number 202 is seen coupled to a Nalco tanker. Nalco Chemicals are a provider of water treatment products. Reliance was to be taken into the Linkman operation as part of the Transport Development Group (TDG).

To prove the point we see two ERF outfits in the Linkman yard in Altrincham. The C Series (167) of Reliance appears to have the fleet colours of Shell Chemicals where the E14 (fleet number 185) is in the TDG Linkman 'Juggler' livery. Both outfits are on the tank cleaning bay. Of note most TDG lorries had identical fleet and registration numbers.

For the carriage of corrosive liquids, we have a four-compartment tank trailer attached to a Leyland Roadtrain (T45) of Linkman (fleet number 406). However, this one was based in the Runcorn, Cheshire, depot. The Hazchem sign on the tank side was a system introduced in the 1970s and is an action code in case of a spillage or mishap.

Another outfit to be seen during the Reliance/TDG transition period is this ERF E10 (fleet number 192) rest cab 6x2 unit of TDG Linkman coupled to a Reliance tandem axle tank trailer. This vehicle was another based and photographed in the Altrincham depot.

A fine Foden 4350 (fleet number 468) with full sleeper cab. Again this is a 6x2 unit, which gave the outfit five axles to comply with gross vehicle weight (G.V.W.) Still on five axles, some outfits had a 4x2 unit but were attached to tri-axle trailers. This example again was in the Altrincham depot.

Showing traces of its parentage to Leyland with a facelifted T45 sleeper cab, this Leyland/DAF 80 six-wheeler (fleet number 742) was contracted to Imperial Chemical Industries (I.C.I.) by Linkman. It has a three-compartment tank body for carrying solvents.

Yet another Linkman vehicle in customer livery. This ERF E10 rest cab (187) was on contract to Burmah and serviced filling station forecourt requirements. We can assume the number on the door (2866) was its previous fleet number prior to the addition of the Linkman 187.

In a later and rather more pleasing Burmah livery at Linkman's we have another 10-litre E Series ERF. It does highlight the popular choice of this make of lorry for not only large fleet users but also smaller operators. The advantages were the availability of reasonably priced spares and the proximity to the manufacturers over in Sandbach.

Fleet number 1304 in the Burmah fleet? This London-registered DAF 2100 six-wheel fuel tanker was in the Altrincham Linkman depot. Whether this ever had a Linkman fleet number is only guesswork as the DAF was soon to be off the fleet.

More mystery? We see here an ERF E10 at a now abandoned filling station on the old A50 in Foston, Derbyshire. This is lettered to Major and would probably have been from the Colwick depot, Nottingham. It has the same livery as Burmah and does actually have a Burmah tank trailer attached. Health and safety does not allow personnel atop the tanks nowadays!

Hercules was a company specialising in printing ink. The company merged later with Ashland Inc., providing a worldwide chemical product service. Linkman had this ERF E10 on contract to them and as can be seen on the Hazchem sign the product carried was deemed 'Low Hazard'.

Another part of the T.D.G. operation was the powder tank division using the name 'Nexus'. The vehicle depicted here though is one that was run by Harris Road Services of Lostock Gralam, Northwich. This company was taken over by T.D.G. and the ERF M16 had been pensioned off ready for disposal.

This E6 ERF of Nexus was captured on film on Sandbach Services en route back to reload at the salt works. The livery adorning the vehicle is for the Salt Union, which is a mining and metals company based in the heart of the salt mines of Cheshire in Winsford.

Not being able to resist an eight-wheeler, the camera caught this ERF E10 in the old yard of Harris Road Services at Lostock Gralam. Another in the nice Salt Union livery, the yard that T.D.G. had taken over was to later become Jack Richards Cheshire Northwich depot.

Over in the Peak District at Hindlow, Buxton, we have a Peakstone lime powder tanker. Part of the Ready Mixed Concrete Group, this Leyland Constructor (T45) eight-wheel vehicle was fleet number 18747 and looked rather 'work worn' when seen one weekend.

Also seen in the Hindlow Quarry of Peakstone, this Foden 4350 4x2 artic was keeping company with its stablemates over a weekend break way back in 1990. Hard to think that the photo was taken over thirty years ago!

Fleet number 27, sporting a personalised registration number, is an ERF E14 artic tanker from Brit-European. The lorry is seen in the old Beech's Garage premises in Hanley, Stoke on Trent. Brit-European originally was Carmans Transport (1924) from neighbouring Scholar Green in the county of Cheshire, and is still going strong today. One major customer is JCB for machinery shipments.

This Seddon Atkinson 301 powder tanker was also seen in Beech's Garage. Apparently, the chassis, which is Stoke on Trent registered, was ex-British Industrial Sand (B.I.S.) and would possibly have operated from the nearby Moneystone Quarry in Oakamoor. It later passed to Febry's of Chipping Sodbury, Gloucestershire, and was awaiting attention at Beech's.

On a very dark and dismal day the author came across this Steyr-cabbed ERF ES6 gas tanker of Freedom LPG from Chesterfield. It was in Cheadle, Staffordshire, and the driver was after directions to a nearby customer. These were gratefully given from the author to the driver in exchange for the photograph!

Bulkhaul of Middlesbrough are involved in the movements of bulk powders, liquids and gases and this fine E Series ERF is seen in the yard in 1993. It is coupled to a trailer carrying a lift off 'tanktainer'. The company specialises in this mode of transport and is a global market leader with over 20,000 deep sea isotanks.

Here we have an ex-Blue Circle Cement Foden S21 (Mickey Mouse) eight-wheel bulk tanker that had been sold onto Harrison Mayer of Meir, Stoke on Trent. Harrison Mayer was a major supplier to the local ceramics industry and were later taken over by Cookson's. The lorry was only used occasionally on internal duties around the factory. Alas, all gone now, and the factory demolished.

This tidy Seddon 16:4 water bowser, of North West Water, was seen at the start of the HCVS Trans-Pennine run in 1990 at Belle Vue, Manchester. It was in fact still available for duty when required. Since then it was sold out of service and converted to a tractor unit and can still be seen on the rally scene.

On contract to Warwick International (Leeds & Mostyn) and seen taking a break at Hilton Park Services (M6) we see one of the well-turned-out fleet of Sayers from Newbury, Berkshire. This Scania 112M, fleet number 85, rejoices in the name *Wessex Volunteer*. The company were taken over by De Rijke, who have their head office in Hull.

Specialist chemical company Manro from Stalybridge, Cheshire, supplies chemicals for use in the detergent and soap manufacturing industries, which, according to the Hazchem sign, are low hazard. This tidy ERF E14 artic was taking a break on Ferrybridge Services back in 1992. The E14 was a very popular choice with many operators at this time.

M.A.N. TGA 26.430 with the D20 common rail engine is from the large milk transport concern J. H. Willis from over in Gresford, Wrexham. This example was on the new Poplar Truck stop in Lymm, Cheshire, in 2010, and, being on six axles, will operate at the maximum G.V.W. allowed.

Back in 1993 a visit to J. H. Willis at their Gresford yard was taken. At the time they were service agents for ERF. Therefore, it was no surprise to see most vehicles were from that manufacturer. This M16 four-wheel single compartment tanker was run by associate company Willmorr Haulage Ltd.

W. Everard & Son were another major user of ERF lorries. This B Series artic was seen on a visit to the yard in North Kyme, Lincolnshire, in 1992. Chassis number 37516 had the Jennings sleeper conversion, which was popular before ERF introduced their own factory-built version.

Not in use at the time, this AEC Mammoth Major Mk5 had only recently been retired by a bus company where it had been used as a fuel bowser. Keen-eyed readers will see that it has the Road Transport Services (R.T.S.) cab with 'suicide' forward opening doors fitted.

Gary Walker from Cromford set up on his own company as Alabaster Bulk Haulage (ABH). The name originated from the road that he lived in at the time! However, it was an appropriate name as alabaster is processed to make plaster powder. This ERF E10 powder tanker is chassis number 55887 and may well have carried the product during its working life.

Always a well-turned-out fleet, Longcliffe Quarries are situated in Brassington, a small village in Derbyshire. Their fine Foden 4300 is a typical example. It is fitted with the Gardner 6LXDT engine, which as the grille badge states produced 270 bhp.

Probably the world's largest packet of Polo mints is seen here behind Nestle Distribution's ERF E14. Fleet number 5075 was seen at the Farm Café on the A17 in Lincolnshire in company with other vehicles from the same firm. They would have been from the factory in York and this café was apparently a regular comfort break for their drivers.

Transporting liquid argon this Seddon Atkinson 4-11 sleeper cab artic of Air Products (A328) was seen just about to leave motorway services. The driver was more than happy to stop for a photo before continuing with his days' work. The transport of Air Products was later taken over by the Wincanton Group.

Now, this photograph of a nice-looking ERF E10 was taken in in 1993 but later on in the book it will be seen again with a previous owner. Owned here at the time by Lakin's from Somerford near Congleton, it was enjoying a weekend break. Keen-eyed readers will no doubt later see its previous livery, which was spotted three years earlier in 1990.

Seen at the Royal Worcester Porcelain works, this DAF 2500 (25.9), of the Cleansing Service Group, was from the nearby Evesham depot and had been to the factory to remove pottery waste slurry. The author had to wait while the job was done before unloading liquid water ground bone from the Leyland Buffalo seen earlier in the book.

Maurice Neild had quite a sizable fleet at one time and did take over the running of the British Coal lorries in the Stoke area. This ERF E14 was in Beech's Garage, the local ERF dealers, for service or repair.

Fleet number 8046 of Esso Petroleum is this Foden 4350, which was captured replenishing the underground fuel tanks at Hilton Park Services on the M6 motorway. How times change. Taken in 1990, the photo shows a row of dipsticks on top of the tanker that the driver would use to show the customer the amount of fuel left. Health and safety does not allow this practice anymore.

An ex-Tankfreight, this lovely looking outfit was used for the carriage of plastic granules. Youngs of Stokesley were based in North Yorkshire and when a call was made to the yard in August 1993 it was nice to see a fleet of ERF vehicles including this E10 4x2 artic.

Long since disappeared from our roads is the Blue Circle Cement livery, which could be spotted from miles away. Now part of Lafarge, fleet number 2477H is a Leyland Roadtrain 17-25, which has a bottom discharge powder tank trailer attached. It is seen parked at the Cauldon Works one weekend many moons ago in 1990.

Back in 2005 the Caldon Canal in Froghall, Staffordshire, saw the start of the restoration of the Uttoxeter arm. With many years of accumulated rubbish Jet Vac Systems (J.V.S.) from Middlesbrough were using this DAF CF to extract the slurry. The Hazchem sign denotes non-dangerous. Of note is the small wheel ahead of the drive axle, which is lowered once loaded and surreptitiously nicknamed pram wheels!

It is amazing what can be found when on your travels. This ex-military AEC Militant 6x6 fuel bowser was ideal to traverse the undulating landscape on sites to refuel the plant equipment. It was seen near to Kegworth on a road construction site in 1993.

Another café, another pitstop. On the A34 in Talke, Staffordshire, was the now demolished Windy Ridge Café. This Leyland Cruiser 16-15 of Edwards of Hull would have been on contract to Ideal Standard from nearby Middlewich, makers of sanitary ware. The vehicle could well have been on its way to collect earthenware 'slop' from the potteries in Stoke.

Delivering heating oil to a local warehouse in Fenton, Stoke on Trent, fleet number 411 is a Leyland Constructor that was operated by fuel distributors UK Petroleum. It is fitted with a rest cab version of the T45 cab, which was designed by Ogle and manufactured by Motor Panels of Coventry.

Presumably the driver of this Foden S80 powder tanker lived in one of the nearby houses in Hanley, Stoke on Trent, as it was often seen there. Joseph Kimberley & Sons from Stoke are a long-established company and operated various types of vehicles over the years. Today they are mostly engaged on waste material removal with skips, etc.

Sporting a full sleeper cab, this Foden S81 artic powder tanker was often parked on this waste ground at the side of the road, near the top of the notorious Swinscoe bank on the A52 close to the Staffordshire/Derbyshire border. Philip Jones was an owner driver running out of local quarries on limestone.

Leyland Octopus with the Ergomatic cab made by Sankey. This eight-wheel fuel tanker was parked for a while just off the A5 near Cannock, Staffordshire. Although still bearing its Amoco livery, it was no longer in service. On the front grille is a Greater London Borough exemption plate, which allowed running in the capital.

As mentioned previously, it's amazing what you can stumble across. This ex-RAF AEC Mammoth Major aircraft refueller was tucked away around the back of a car sales garage in Hanley. Nobody on site knew any details but it is thought that it might have been purchased as a source of spares for another such vehicle now preserved.

Not in a normal working environment in the middle of a field, this Foden 4350 (S10 Mk4 cab) 4x2 artic was seen at a truck show in Grappenhall, Warrington, in 1991 when only a couple of years old. As can be seen on the headboard, the outfit transported salt.

Parked out of use in a compound, a photograph of this vehicle was managed by poking the camera lens though a fence. One of two on site, this Seddon 16:4 fuel tanker of L & W Jones Fuels was later purchased and used as a bowser on internal duties on the old Shelton Steelworks.

A chocoholic's dream? This ERF C40 (day cab) artic with a Rolls-Royce engine was operated by the Caxton Chocolate Company of Wood Green, London. A tank full of liquid chocolate would certainly satisfy lots of appetites! The vehicle was seen on the now defunct Congleton cattle market one weekend back in 1984.

Part of the Tudor Griffiths Group from over Ellesmere in Shropshire, this smart ES8 240 ERF with Steyr cab was seen in Beech's Garage having been in for a service. Fleet number C64 was in the associate company livery of Swan Petroleum.

Caradon Twyford had factories at Etruria, Stoke on Trent, and Alsager, Cheshire. They manufactured sanitary ware and this Leyland Bison2 six-wheel tanker was used to transport clay slurry. It was seen in 1989 at the Etruria factory not long before it closed down.

Badged as a Marshal, this AEC, judging by the length of the chassis, must have been a six-wheel rigid cut down. It is certainly too long for it to be a Mercury. Used on internal duty at the Air Products depot in Stoke, it was quite a find as access was not normally permitted due to the nature of the business of flammable gas production.

ERF E14 6x2 twin steer artic fuel tanker seen having replenished the storage tanks on the busy Woodall Services on the M1 in South Yorkshire. The vehicle, on contract to Shell UK, came from the Farnworth, Bolton, fleet of long-established haulier Hipwood & Grundy and bore fleet number 109. The company was engaged on all types of transport and closed in the 1990s.

Road contractor vehicles often have long and arduous lives. This AEC Mercury tar tanker of Tarmac Ltd was first registered in 1975/76. It was still in service at fifteen years old when seen in 1990 just off the Worcester southbound junction 7 on the M5. The link road was undergoing works to improve traffic flow.

When doing casual driving the author nearly always kept the camera in the cab. A break on Wardley Industrial Estate in Manchester for a bacon sandwich and coffee saw this ageing B Series ERF eight-wheel tanker pull up. Again, longevity prevailed as this was seventeen years old at the time.

Foden 4350 of B. A. Jenner (Bill) who was a contract haulier for Rugby Cement (fleet number 6850). Although a working vehicle, it was actually an entry in the Classic Commercial Motor Show (CCMS) 1994 when it was held at the BP Truckstop, Rugby. Keen observers will note the nameplate in the window of Lady Truckers founder Ilona Richards.

The Volvo FL range for some reason earned the nickname 'Wendy house'. This example owned by William Rainford Ltd from Doncaster was often parked on this wasteland at Earl Sterndale near Buxton. The driver was presumably based near there and maybe carried bulk powders from the nearby quarries in the area.

A relatively small fleet, but one that has been around for many years, is Walsh's from Haslington, Crewe. At almost twenty years old, this ERF with LV cab was still giving excellent service in 1992. Mr Walsh spoke highly for the marque and was loyal to both ERF and Foden, who of course were quite close in nearby Sandbach.

Another fine-looking powder tanker on the Walsh's fleet in 1992 was the youngster in the yard, namely an ERF E12, which was fitted with a Rolls-Royce 'Eagle TX' engine. It is often seen in and around Cheshire and Derbyshire running limestone from the area's quarries.

Coupled to a chemicals tank trailer this day cabbed C Series ERF was seen taking a break at the Junction 23 Truckstop in Shepshed, Leicestershire. Imperial Tankers was founded in 1989 and its head office was in Scunthorpe. The company was bought from the Hargreaves Group by Suttons in 2014.

Local to the author, Stoddard's Fuel Services Ltd have been involved for many years in the transport business with a mix of tippers, coaches and tankers. The tankers are now the mainstay and this AEC Marshal, back in 1991, was used to store buffer stocks of heating oil. Conoco is the trade name of the Continental Oil Company.

A well workworn S10 (Mk3) cabbed Foden S106 with a double drive rear bogie on powder tank work for I.F. & J. Bolshaw from the small village of Rainow near Macclesfield, Cheshire. The photograph was taken a number of years ago on the M6 service area at Hilton Park.

A smart-looking ERF E12 (rest cab) in the livery of NWF Fuels Ltd. This was a division of North West Farmers from Wardle near Nantwich. However, it is most likely to have been based in the Stoke depot as it was delivering domestic heating oil in the small area of Cheadle known as Trimpos.

This vehicle started life with Rugby Portland Cement (fleet number 490) before finding its way into the Derbyshire hills and service with the late Roy Melland. The Foden Haulmaster (S10 Mk1 cab) later got sold to Bailey Bros in Stoke on Trent where it was converted to a tipper and used on the Croxden Gravel contract.

MAN 30.291 (sleeper cab) of Lock from Headcorn, Kent. Mounted with a five-compartment tank, the vehicle was quite far from home as it was caught on film taking a break on the Hilton Park service area in 1994. Of interest is the Brunswick Lion emblem on the grille that relates to MAN taking over Bussing from Brunswick, Germany, in 1971.

Sometimes, when out and about, stumbling across such a gem as this Leyland Steer integral tanker necessitates a photo, even when conditions are not ideal. The vehicle was out of use on a small airfield in Henstridge and is quite rare as it was one of a range of such vehicles made by Thompson Bros of Bilston in Staffordshire.

Peninsular and Oriental, better known as P & O, were the operators of this ERF E10 artic three-compartment tanker that carried fleet number 494. It was caught on film on the southbound side of the M6 services in Sandbach a number of years back in 1993.

And another ERF E10 on Sandbach Services, this time a reasonable distance away from its home town of Basingstoke, Hampshire. It was operated by Berk Limited and used for the carriage of liquid sulphur, a versatile product used in making acid, rubber products, detergents, fertilizers and in petroleum refining.

Foden Fleetmaster S10 Mk2 full sleeper cab of Roger Bettley Ltd. The vehicle is pictured at home in the yard at Sandbach not very far from where the vehicle was made. The Hazchem sign indicates the tank is for the carriage of hydrochloric acid.

ERF E12 TX 6x2 unit of Bitmac Transport Ltd from Scunthorpe was captured taking a break at the Tamworth Services, which is situated near the A5/M42. Bitmac is actually a product similar to asphalt and has no tar but bitumen in the make-up, along with fillers, and offers a cheaper option to road surfacing than asphalt.

A Stoke on Trent-registered Seddon Atkinson 2-11 would no doubt have been supplied by Mainline Trucks of Tunstall to Halso UK Fuels Ltd. This vehicle was in the old British Coal yard at Staffordshire House, Fenton, one weekend. The nearest depot to Stoke was Ashbourne in Derbyshire, so why it happened to be here is pure guesswork.

A train journey from Stoke to Crewe saw the author spotting this Leyland Octopus tanker in the distance. Having made a mental note of the location, the vehicle was tracked down to an opencast site at Peacocks Hay, Talke, where it was in use as a bowser. It still bore the livery of its previous owner, Phillips 66 Petroleum.

Another Seddon Atkinson 2-11 fuel tanker and almost identical to the previous Halso vehicle. This one was actually at Mainline Trucks, the Seddon Atkinson dealers for the area. No doubt Fox Petroleum from Greater Manchester had taken the vehicle in for service or repair.

The name *Maurice* is just discernible on the driver's door of this E6 ERF (rest cab) gas tanker of Transgas. No doubt the driver took pride in his vehicle with such an adornment. The vehicle was seen not far from the Stoke depot in Cheadle, Staffordshire.

This Scania 4 Series artic of Tankfreight (H0928) is seen here having the tank purged at the Reg Morris tank wash facility in Kilworth, Leicestershire. On contract to Vinamul Polymers from Warrington, who made chemicals and paint, it would no doubt be getting cleaned prior to its next load to stop any cross-contamination.

Also at Kilworth in 1999 this ageing Leyland Bison 6-wheel vacuum tank of Reg Morris was seen. At twenty years old it was still in use in and around the yard and would serve as a useful vehicle to empty storage tanks and to provide buffer storage.

The Armco barriers on the side of this tank trailer obviously indicates that protection is a must for dangerous cargos – in this instance liquid sodium. O. B. Transport (Offley Bros) from Ellesmere Port had this work-worn Leyland Roadtrain on the fleet and it is seen here on Markham Moor Services taking a breather in 1992.

Solrec is a company specialising in solvent recovery. This Seddon Atkinson Strato was on contract to them and was actually owned by the famous W & J Riding from Longridge, Preston. The vehicle was named *Flamboyant* and was fleet number 31. The company was taken over by the Transport Development Group and was one of the few that retained the original livery.

Here we see the famous W & J Riding livery. Back in the 1970s Tom Riding decided to not only have fleet numbers but also to name all the fleet. True Ridings liveries, as seen here on Seddon Atkinson Strato (fleet number 77, *Sir Tristram*), also have the slogan 'THE BEST IN THE LONG RUN'. The vehicle is coupled a 'tanktainer' trailer (fleet number 119).

Fleet number 74 Pentland Firth on the hymn sheet is another W & J Riding vehicle that was in customer livery. ERF E10 (rest cab), a bulk cement tanker, was on for Ready Mixed Concrete (RMC). This shot was taken in the yard in 1993 and a lot has changed since then.

Townson Bros (Fuel Services) are based on Pendle Industrial Estate in Chatburn, Clitheroe, Lancashire, and this tidy DAF 75.360 was seen in the yard one weekend in 2007. Behind closed gates, a shot of the vehicle was taken over the gates by standing in the car boot!

Arla Foods is a big player in the transport and processing of milk products. This Scania 114G 380 (day cab) eight-wheeler had a self-steer rear axle and was seen in their yard when on a visit to the Giggleswick Dairy in 2007.

Fleet number 31 of British Salt Ltd from Middlewich, Cheshire, was this Foden 2200 four-wheel vehicle. This has the narrow version of the S10 cab. At the time (1992) British Salt was part of Staveley Industries PLC. The yard on Cledhill Lane always had a good selection of vehicles to photograph.

Also on Cledhill Lane was this Foden S108R with the S10 Mk3 sleeper cab. Rejoicing in the name *Princess Diane* (fleet number 36), this was enjoying a weekend break as the photo was taken one Sunday just prior to the Christmas holiday on 19 December 1993. British Salt were loyal customers to the local manufacturers with both Foden and ERF on station.

This Foden S108 (S10 Mk2) with a Rolls-Royce 265 engine is seen in a lay-by on the A57 Manchester to Sheffield road on Snake Pass. Fleet number 30 *Snooty Fox* had followed the author out of Manchester to pull in for a break at the tea van. The author's vehicle rear end and concrete manhole covers are just visible to the right.

No self-respecting lorry enthusiast could miss the sight of a Sam Longson vehicle. The livery could be spotted miles away but on this occasion a visit to the yard in 1990 saw the yard shunter (788) in charge of a tank trailer that had just been freshly painted. Seddon Atkinson 401 was looking a little worse for wear but was still a useful tool.

A prime example of Sam Longson's fleet is this ERF E10 (fleet number 117) with rest cab. An eight-wheel rigid powder tanker, it was one of a large fleet that was primarily ERF. The company were engaged on bulk powders and liquids, with local quarry work on limestone being the mainstay.

However, being based in Chapel-en-le-Frith meant that the Cheshire salt mines were not too far away and they also provided work. Yet another ERF E10 (fleet number 849) eight-wheeler, the vehicle is in the Imperial Chemical Industries (ICI) salt livery, which includes the Longson name.

Seddon Atkinson 401 (fleet number 906) was one of a few of this marque on station at the time (1990). Keen-eyed readers will no doubt realise that the fleet and registration numbers of Longson's were the same. This particular motor was contracted to ICI Cement.

Chassis number 55763 was one of the main players in the Longson fleet. A large number of this specification (ERF E14) were on the fleet and gave excellent service. The sight of Sam Longson's vehicles plying their trade along the roads are now sorely missed by all.

Sellers and Kent were well known among lorry enthusiasts, based in the small village of Ilam in the heart of Dovedale. Later on, Sellers set up on his and Tony Kent moved to Ashbourne to set up AK Transport. This fine Foden S83 eight-wheel powder tanker of Sellers (2) was seen on the now defunct Ashbourne lorry park in 1987.

Another one of Sellers of Ilam in Ashbourne lorry park was this Foden 4350 artic. Unfortunately, as in a good many cases the lorry park here was closed down by the environmentalists and the ground has now been redeveloped. Thus, a valuable facility for not only locals but overnight vehicles that were in the area was lost.

New to Shirley's Transport Ltd in 1985, this ERF C Series (fleet number 111) with sleeper cab was in the John Wyatt of Leeds livery. Used for the carriage of oils and fats, it is coupled to an insulated tank trailer to keep the cargo fluid. By 1994 the tractor unit had been sold and was added to the Bassett's of Tittensor fleet.

What could be better for the enthusiast than this excellent Volvo F88 of Shirley's Transport? Fleet number 84 *Grace* was new in May 1975 as a 4x2 unit. Later on, it was refurbished and a lift up tag axle added to reconfigure the unit to 6x2. A fine example of a well-kept fleet, the vehicle, although dismantled, still exists and awaits restoration.

The Volvo F10 and F12 tractor units were much favoured by Shirley's. Several of these joined the fleet and gave excellent service. This F12 (fleet number 118) was coupled to a highly polished insulated tank trailer and seen in the yard in 1997. The unit was eventually sold for export.

After running mainly Volvos for a while Shirley's tried other makes and this fine looking six-axle outfit is headed up by a DAF 95XF 480. It was one of a batch added to the fleet in 1999 and received number 180. It was run for approximately six years before being sold off.

Another marque that made inroads into the Shirley fleet was the Swedish manufacturer Scania. Sporting fleet number 240, Scania 124L 470 (Topline) was on frontline tanker operations and proved to be an excellent choice for the job. How shiny is that tank!

Another make that was tried with Shirley's was Mercedes. This Actros 2546 (fleet number 255) with full sleeper cab was three years old when seen in the yard in 2006. Nearly all Shirley's vehicles had fleet numbers but not all were named as is the case here.

Not immediately apparent as it is in the customer livery of F. F. Man Feed Products is this Volvo FH12. Shirley's fleet number 163 gives a small clue to the ownership. A few vehicles on the fleet received this livery and were used on the animal fats feed contract.

Somewhat of an interloper, this Iveco Eurotech Cursor 430 (Fleet number 206 *Cyclone Zoe*) proved to be a reliable performer so the name on the sun visor may be very appropriate. The vehicle very often ran on the Continent. Again, only a limited number of this make made it onto the fleet.

Still in business today, the fine fleet of F.R. Somerset from Chapel-en-le-Frith run on general haulage and as seen here they also run bulk powder tankers under the name Combs Valley Tankers Ltd. This ERF was a typical vehicle being a 6x2 unit coupled to a tandem axle trailer.

Yet another name that has disappeared from the UK roads is Steetley. Named after a small hamlet near Worksop where they had a quarry the company grew and had several UK operations. This Foden S108 (S10 MK3 cab), fleet number 723, was parked up for the weekend at Dowlow Quarry near Buxton in 1990.

Likewise enjoying the weekend break was this Foden S104 artic powder tanker. At the time of writing (2020) the quarry in Dowlow is operated by Omya/Lafarge Aggregates. Steetley was taken over by Redland Industries in 1992. Both names are now a thing of the past.

Fleet number 725 on the hymn sheet at Steetley was this rather tired-looking Leyland Constructor (T45 cab) eight-wheel rigid powder tanker. Presumably it was from Dowlow but on this occasion, it was parked on some waste land in Cobridge, Stoke on Trent.

This vacuum tanker of Severn Trent Water Authority (fleet number 3030) was seen at Charnwood Truck Centre, Shepshed, on 21 March 1992. A Foden 4300 with the S10 Mk4 cab, one can only guess why it was at a Renault dealer's premises!

Back in 1991 a visit was made to the Perseverance flour mill of Thomas Sugden, who at the time had been absorbed into the Allied Mills empire. For the enthusiast it was a pleasure to find nearly all the vehicles were from the ERF stable. This C Series 4x2 unit (fleet number 4) with a day cab was parked up one Saturday after a week's hard work.

One of the author's all-time favourite photos, this ERF C31 rigid 8 flour tanker (fleet number 7) is seen in the compound at Sugden's Brighouse premises. The imposing mill can be seen in the background, the massive silos being visible from miles around. Unfortunately, the company closed in 1997.

Proudly displaying the Union Jack, which was a theme started for the Queens Jubilee in 1977, this Leyland Freighter 16-17 (fleet number 3009) of Suttons (St Helens) was seen in their Widnes depot in 1993. As it was a vacuum tank, it may be assumed that it could have been a standby vehicle to assist in transferring loads or maybe to empty waste storage tanks.

Presumably this tank trailer may have been for the carriage of a caustic substance such as acid or sodium, etc. The Hazchem code of 2Z does not actually determine what may be carried, it is only for the authorities to distinguish how to deal with any incident. This ERF E Series (fleet number 3578) was another vehicle stationed at Suttons' Widnes depot.

Foden 4320 tractor unit is another vehicle with the S10 Mk4 cab. However, in 1992 the cab had been restyled by Foden's to create this more modern design. Fleet number 4062 of Suttons was yet another captured in the yard at Widnes on a visit in 1993.

In contrast to the previous photograph we see here the earlier S10 Mk4 cab on a Suttons Foden 4350 that was in the Shell Chemicals livery. Fleet number 3840 is seen at Widnes. On the front bumper the London Borough Exemption Scheme plate can be seen, which allowed the vehicle to traverse the capital under certain conditions.

Tardis Environmental UK Ltd from Willenhall operated this vacuum tanker based on a Leyland DAF 85 320 (day cab). It was captured near the author's home one lunchtime, and it had apparently been called in to deal with a problem with a nearby stream/drain blockage.

Yet again, another well-known livery that has long since gone is Tilcon (Tilling Construction). This Foden 4350 with a full S10 Mk4 sleeper cab is in the later livery and is seen parked at Ashbourne Airfield Industrial Estate in 1992, a yard shared at the time with AK Transport.

An earlier S10 Mk1 cab is seen here on Foden Haulmaster rigid 8 tanker. The vehicle does actually show a fleet number whereas on the previous vehicle it appears to be missing. Tilling Holdings are a large concern with many interests and its origins go all the way back to 1846.

Although registered in Staffordshire, this artic vacuum tanker was seen in the UK Waste depot in Widnes, Cheshire. Fleet number T96 is a Foden 4350 4x2 unit and has the S10 Mk4 cab, which is the low-roof sleeper version.

Keeping company with the Foden's at UK Waste was several Leyland DAF vehicles including this Constructor eight-wheeler. Being a Saturday quite a few vehicles in the yard were having routine maintenance carried out. The fitter at the rear must have been a bit shy as he turned his head on seeing the camera!

WG Tankers (Waterhouses Garage) of Waterhouses, Staffordshire, are involved in the sales, service and repair of tankers of all types. They have grown over the years and the business also includes tank hire. This Leyland Roadtrain was used by them to shunt trailers in the yard and to a nearby storage facility. The yellow paint suggests an ex-Blue Circle motor.

A few years later we see another Waterhouses Garage shunter, this time a DAF CF 85.410 6x2 unit fitted with the 'pram' wheels in front of the drive axle. These wheels would be lowered onto the road when the vehicle was fully loaded.

Apparently, this vehicle was used on internal duties at Longcliffe Quarry in Brassington, Derbyshire. It was seen one weekend at Waterhouses Garage where it had been admitted for minor surgery! A sign of the times and to comply with health and safety is the catwalk on top of the tank with fold down handrails.

William Whyte had a sizable fleet based on the old Airfield Industrial Estate in Ashbourne, Derbyshire. A sign of the times (1990) is the '19' number on the front of the cab, which indicates the CB channel that the drivers were using. This ageing Foden Haulmaster was still returning a good day's work even at ten years old.

Another rigid eight-wheel tanker of William Whyte seen on the visit in 1990. This Foden was almost new at the time. With the S10 Mk4 cab, this 4300, apart from the aforementioned '19' logo, also had the drivers 'handle' of Weeble written on the nearside front.

Whyte's also ran articulated bulk powder tankers like this Foden S106 double drive outfit. As in the previous photograph we have the drivers 'handle' of Atomatic showing. Unfortunately, this is another company that has long since gone.

A link with William Whyte was J. Whyte, William's father. He ran this ERF E10 bulk powder tanker from a small yard in the town of Ashbourne. *Yogi Bear*, as it is named, appeared earlier in the book when it had been sold to Lakin.

Wincanton have been a major player in the transport world for a long time. A visit was undertaken in 1993 to the main depot in Wincanton, Somerset. Unusual for a Wincanton vehicle, this one had a fleet number (B743) whereas most vehicles were actually named. This ERF ES6 milk tanker with the Steyr cab was still in the old livery.

Seen on a bay in Wincanton, *River Tutt* was the name given to this ERF E14 artic milk tanker, another vehicle in the old livery. At the time of the author's visit they were in the process of introducing a new colour scheme.

Here we actually have a mix and match outfit as the ERF E12 (River Burn) 4x2 unit is in the new livery and the tri-axle tank trailer has yet to undergo a visit to the paint shop. The premises in Wincanton has got excellent facilities to look after the vehicles.

As a major player it is no surprise to see Wincanton vehicles in customer livery. This Leyland Freighter gives little away as it is in full Corn Products Company United Kingdom Ltd (CPC) livery. The company produces starch products at Trafford Park and was formed in 1929. Fleet number 50 presumably is a CPC allocation. The Wincanton name *Elk* appears on the door.

Another company situated on the Airfield Industrial Estate in Ashbourne is W.R. Wood Haulage Ltd. This eight-wheel Volvo FL7 three-compartment bulk powder tanker was seen on a later visit to the area in June 2000. The livery is similar to a company they took over.

To make the connection we have C. Webster & Sons' Scammell Routeman Mk3. Originally from Wirksworth, on takeover the vehicles were transferred the short distance to Wood's yard in Ashbourne where this photo was taken.

Finally, another of Websters, this time a Leyland Constructor 30-19, which was often parked on a spur road just outside the village of Wirksworth. One can only assume the driver lived nearby. However, the photograph was actually taken prior to the takeover by Wood's so it was on home territory.